Tracing my ABC's

BY DRESSED IN SHEETS

I hope this book makes your little one an outstanding writer now and for the years to come. Thank you very much for what you do for the children of today.

Name:

Aa

Name: _______________________________

Words starting with  **Aa**

_____ nchor

_____ pple

_____ corn

_____ nt

Color the letter **Aa**

b A C

a c A

A B a

I found the letter **Aa** _______ times.

Name: ____________________________

Aa

Word Search

anchor
napple
tacorn

anchor   acorn

apple   ant

Draw a line to help letter A get to letter B.

Name: _______________

Bb

B B B B B B B B B B B B

b b b b b b b b b b b b b

Words starting with **Bb**

_______ all

_______ alloon

_______ ow

_______ ag

Name: _______________________________

Color the letter **Bb**

b A B

a C

b B A

a

I found the letter **Bb** _____________ times.

Name: _______________________________

Bb

Word Search

a b a l l r a
b a l l o o n t
g b o w l a

ball   balloon

bow   bag

Name:

Draw a line to help letter B get to letter C.

Name: ___________________________

Cc

Words starting with **Cc**

_______ ow

_______ at

_______ ake

_______ lock

Color the letter **Cc**

C C C

a C A

C B C

I found the letter **Cc** ________ times.

Name: _______________

Cc

Word Search

c l o c k
a c a k e
t g c o w

cow   cat

cake   clock

Draw a line to help letter C get to letter D.

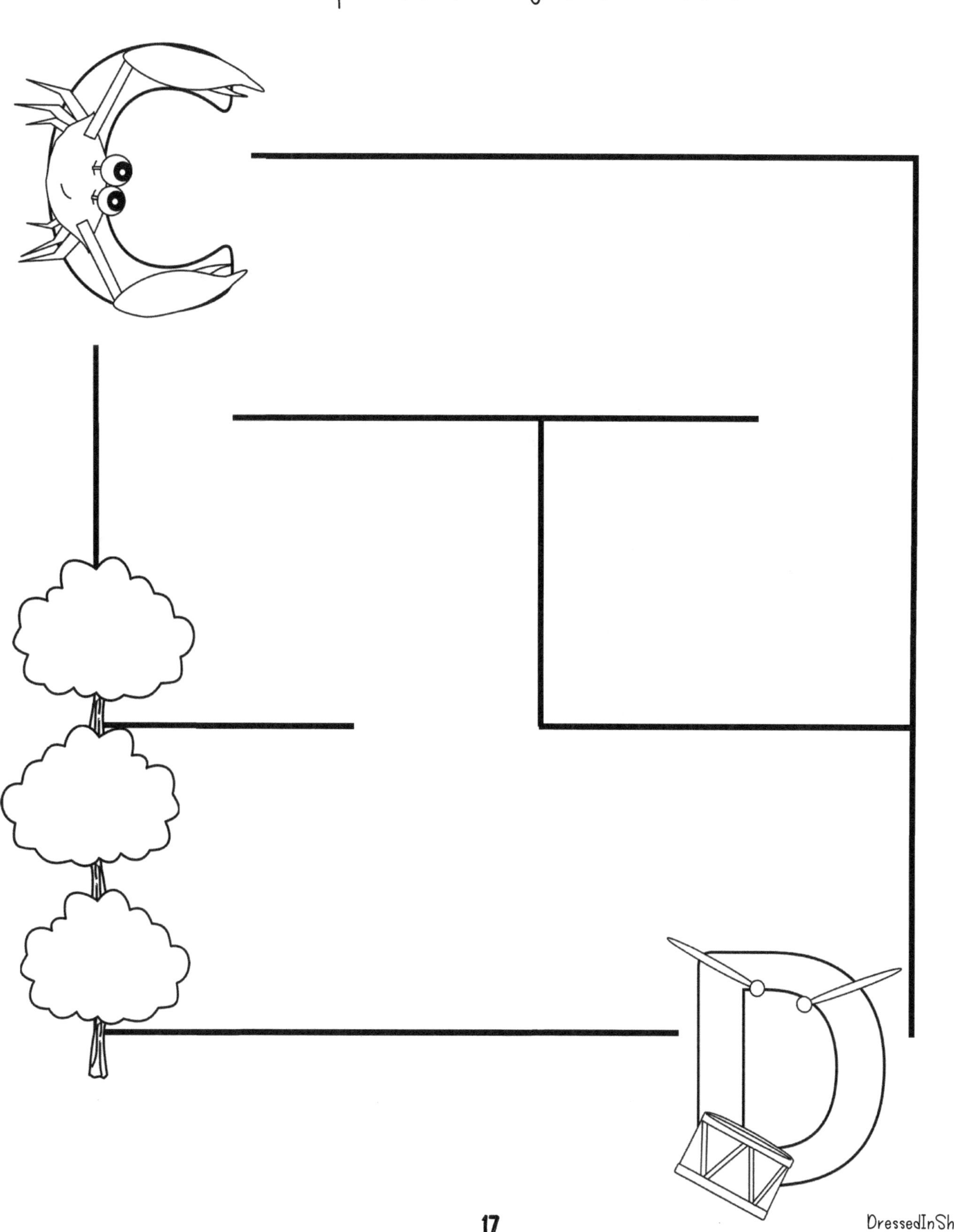

Dd

Name: ___________________

Words starting with 

_____ aisy

_____ og

_____ ice

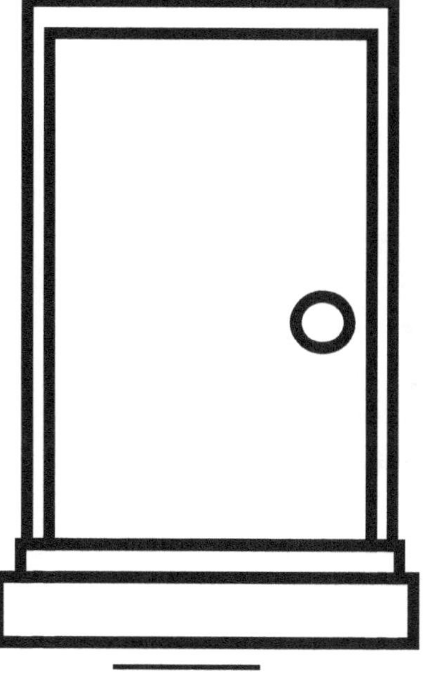

_____ oor

Name: _______________________________________

Color the letter  **Dd**

e   D   F

d   B   f

E   A   D

I found the letter **Dd** ________ times.

Name: _______________

Dd

Word Search

d o o r k d
o d i c e o
d a i s y g

daisy   dog

dice   door

Draw a line to help letter D get to letter E.

Name:

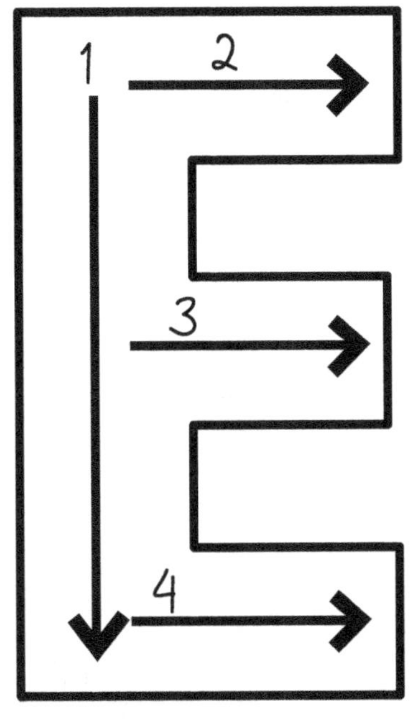
Ee
1
2
3
4

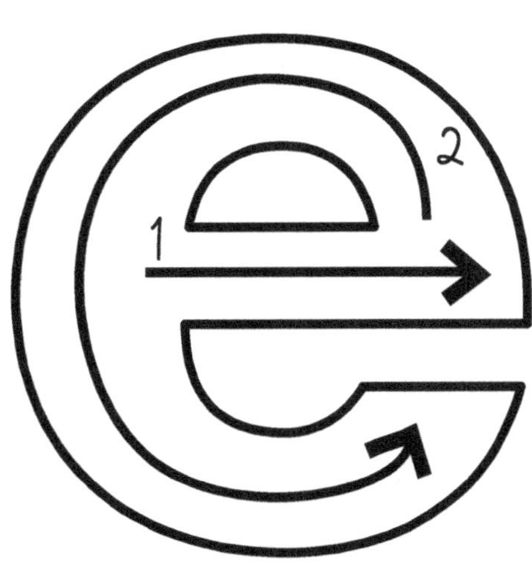
1
2

Name: ____

Words starting with **Ee**

___________ gg

___________ arth

___________ nvelope

___________ ight

Name: _______________________________

Color the letter **Ee**

I found the letter **Ee** _____________ times.

Ee

Word Search

envelope
Earthozg
eightgag

egg   Earth

eight   envelope

Draw a line to help letter E get to letter F.

Name:
Ff

Name: _______________________

Words starting with **Ff**

_____ lower

_____ ish

_____ ruit

_____ ingers

Color the letter **Ff**

I found the letter **Ff** _______ times.

Name: _______________

Ff

Word Search

f l o w e r
f d f i s h
f i n g e r
a f r u i t

flower   fruit

fish   finger

Draw a line to help letter F get to letter G.

Name: _______________________

Gg

Words starting with 

____ lue

____ ift

____ host

____ iraffe

Name: ______________________________

Color the letter **Gg**

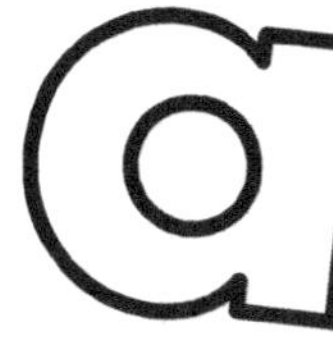

I found the letter **Gg** __________ times.

Gg

Word Search

g i r a f f e
l n i g i f t
u i n g e r a
e g h o s t e

glue   ghost

gift   giraffe

Draw a line to help letter G get to letter H.

Hh

Words starting with Hh

____ and

____ ouse

____ eart

____ orse

Name: _______________________________

Color the letter **Hh**

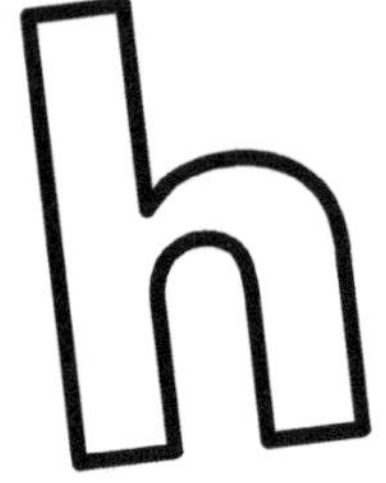

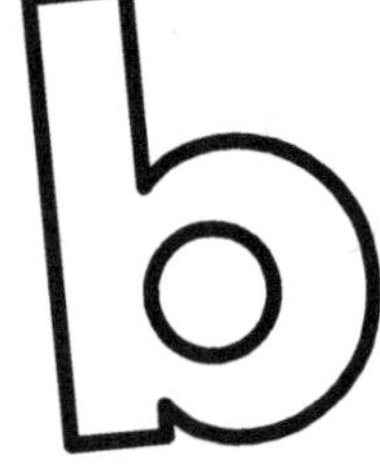

I found the letter **Hh** _______________ times.

Name:

Hh

Word Search

```
h a n d k d
o h o r s e
h e a r t g
a h o u s e
```

hand   house

heart   horse

Draw a line to help letter H get to letter I.

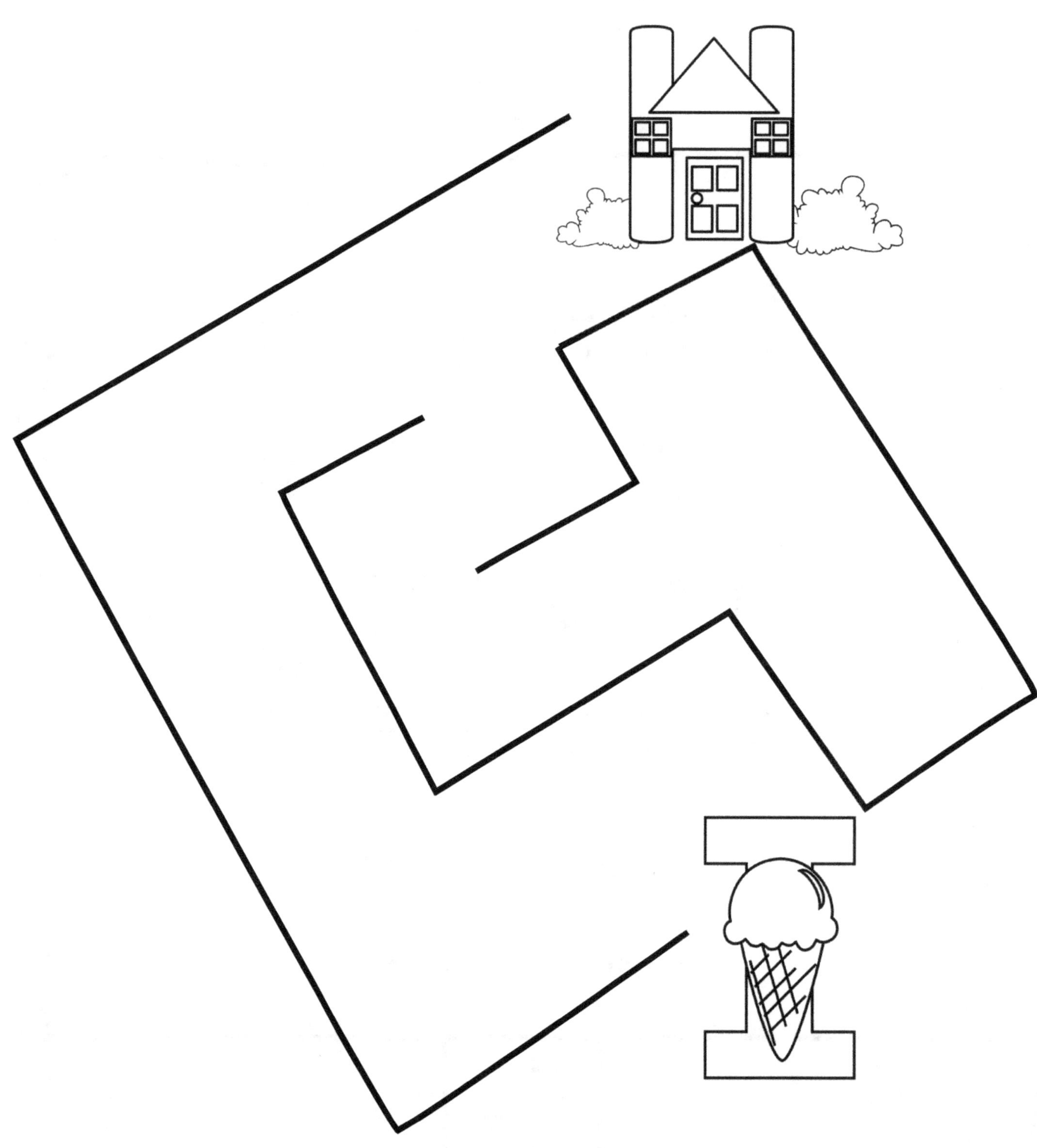

I i

Name: ______________________

Words starting with **I i**

_____ ce cream

_____ gloo

_____ ce

_____ sland

Color the letter **I i**

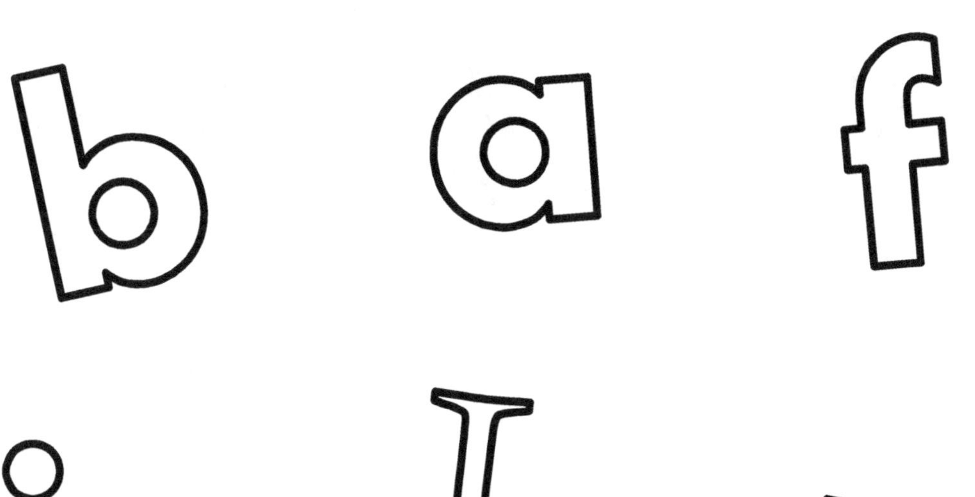

I found the letter **I i** _______ times.

I i

Word Search

ice cream   igloo

ice   island

Draw a line to help letter I get to letter J.

Name: _______________________

J j

Words starting with  J j

____ ar

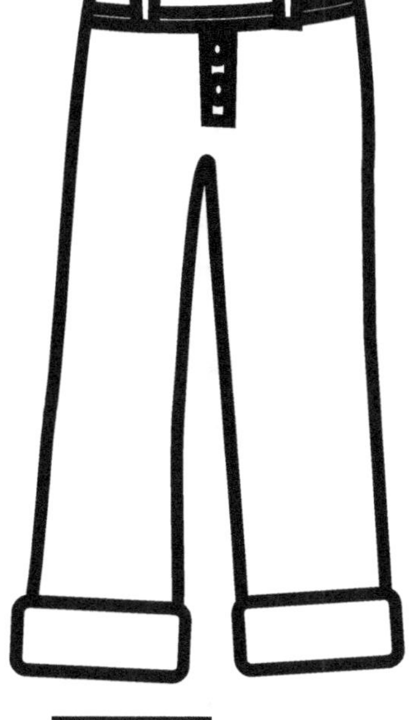

____ eans

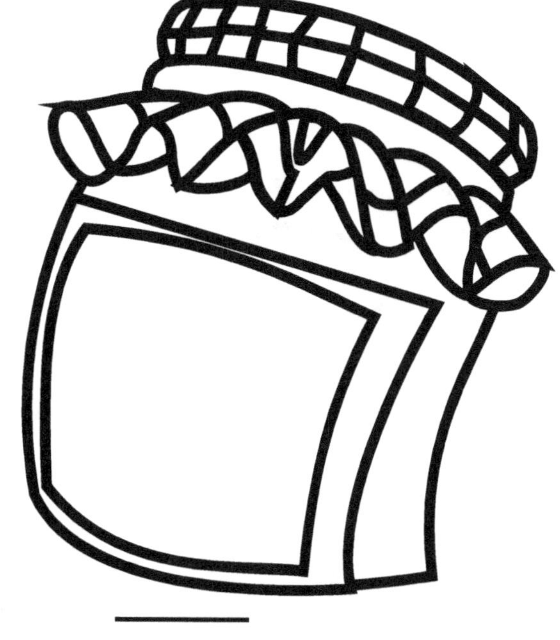

____ am

____ uice

Name: _______________________________

Color the letter **J j**

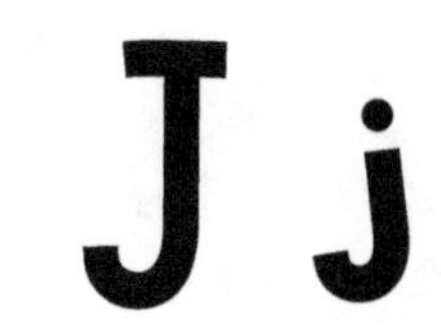

I found the letter **J j** _______ times.

J j

Word Search

j e a n s r j
a j a m o o a
j u i c e l r

jar   jeans

jam   juice

Name: _______________________________

Draw a line to help letter J get to letter K.

Kk

Name: _______________________

Words starting with  **Kk**

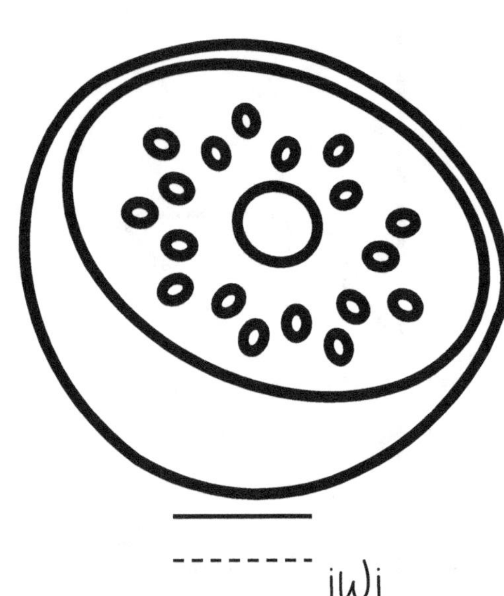

____ iwi

____ ing

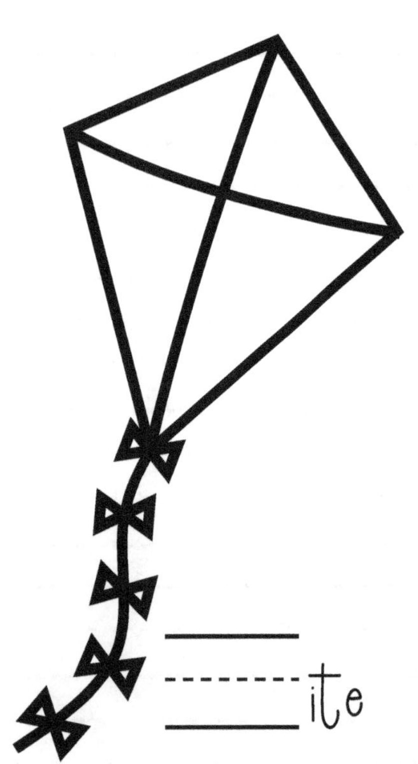

____ ite

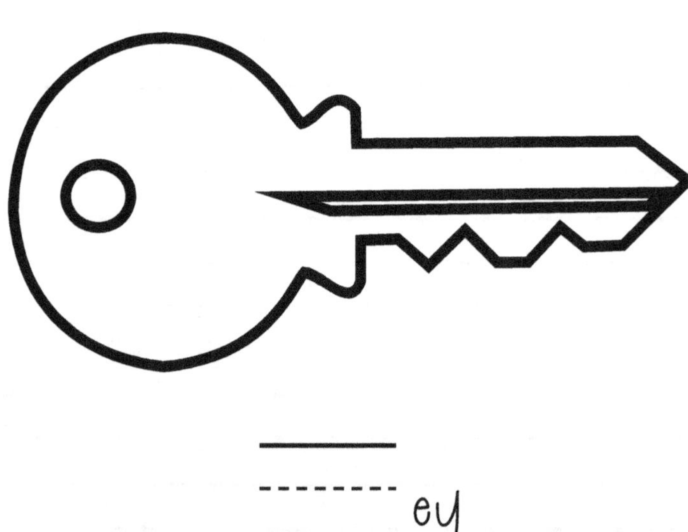

____ ey

Name: ____

Color the letter **Kk**

I found the letter **Kk** _____________ times.

Kk

Word Search

f l k i n g
k i w i s h
f i k i t e
k e y u i t

kiwi   kite

king   key

Draw a line to help letter K get to letter L.

LI

Name: _______________________

Words starting with **Ll**

___ emon

___ ion

___ amp

___ eaf

Name: _______________________________________

Color the letter 

I found the letter  __________ times.

Name:

Ll

Word Search

l e m o n l
i l e a f a
o i k i t m
n e y u i p

lemon   lion

lamp   leaf

Name: _______________________

Draw a line to help letter L get to letter M.

Name: _______________________________

Mm

M m

M M M M M M M M

m m m m m m m m m m

Name: _______________________________

Words starting with  **Mm**

___ ilk

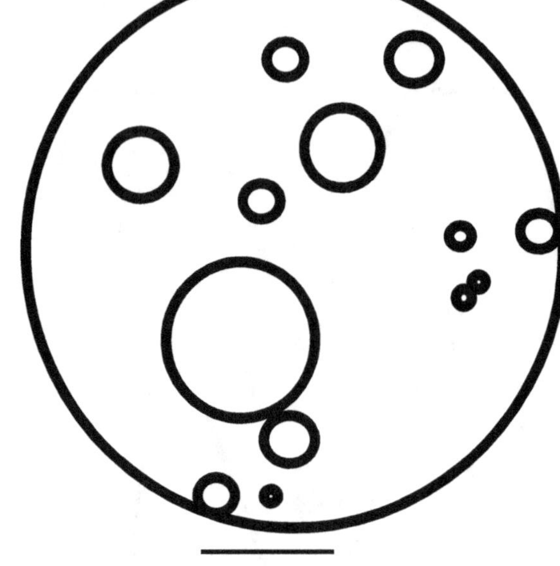

___ oon

___ ug

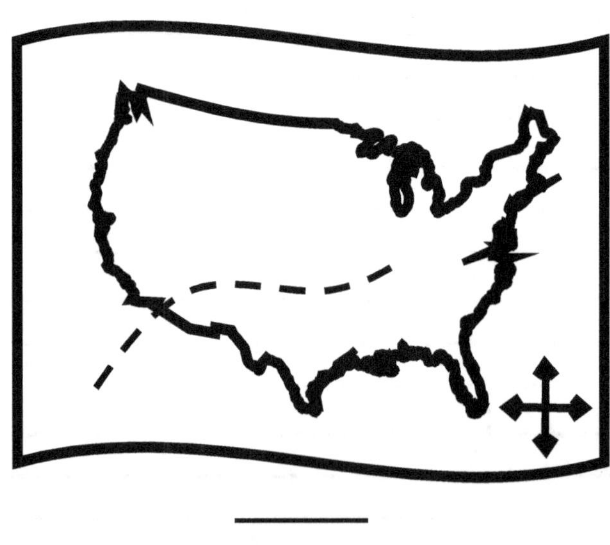

___ ap

Name: _______________________________

Color the letter **Mm**

k M m

h a c

e m f

I found the letter **Mm** _______ times.

Mm

Word Search

m o o n
i m u g
l a k i
k p y u

milk   moon

mug   map

Name: _______________________

Draw a line to help letter M get to letter N.

Nn

N

N N N N N N N N N N

n n n n n n n n n n n

Words starting with **Nn**

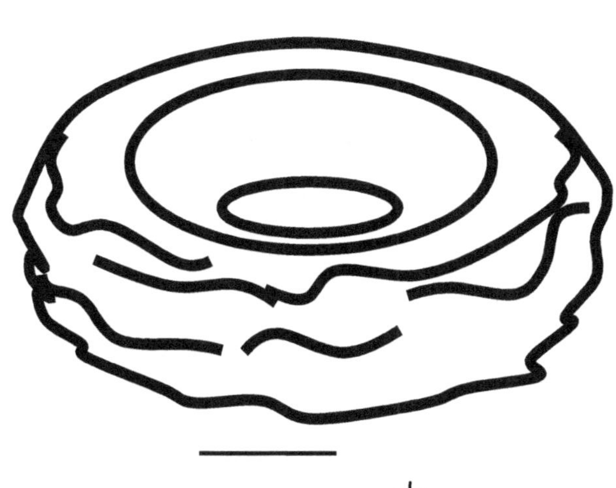

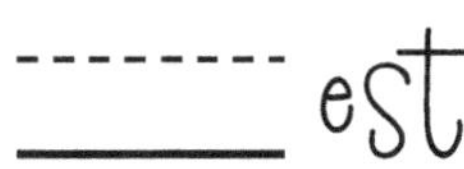

____est

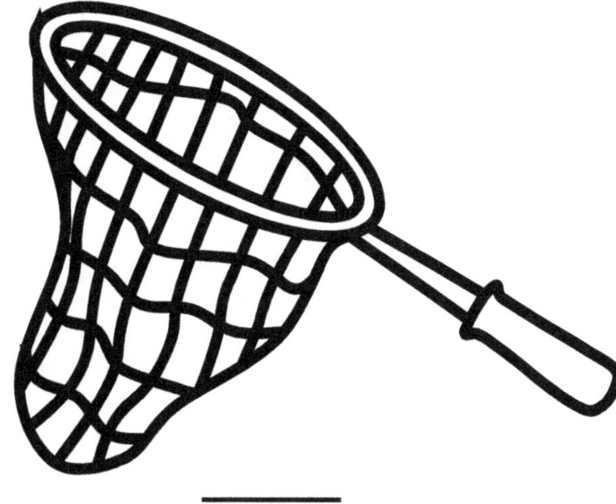

____et

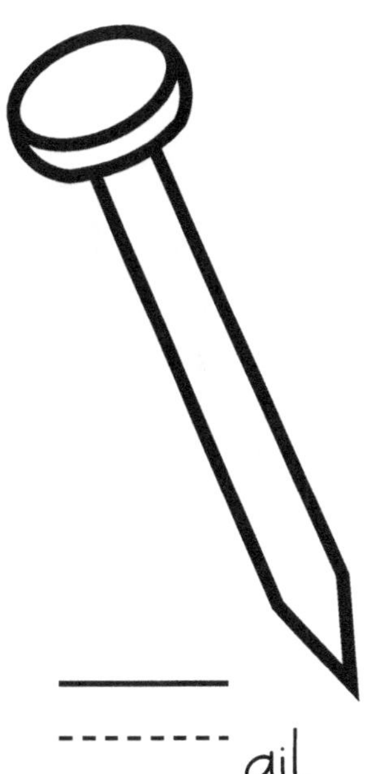

____ail

____ine

Name: _______________________________

Color the letter 

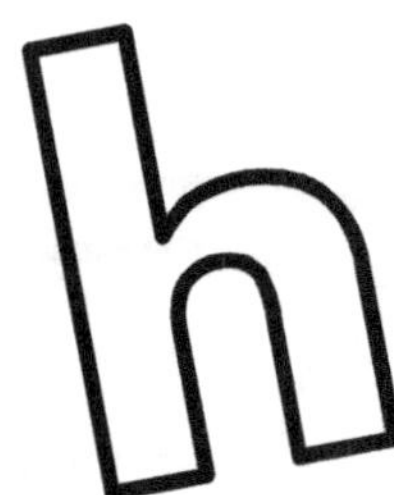

I found the letter  __________ times.

Nn

Word Search

nest   nail

net   nine

Name: _______________________

Draw a line to help letter N get to letter O.

Name:

Oo

Name: _______________________

Words starting with Oo

_______ wl

_______ val

_______ range

_______ pen

Color the letter 

  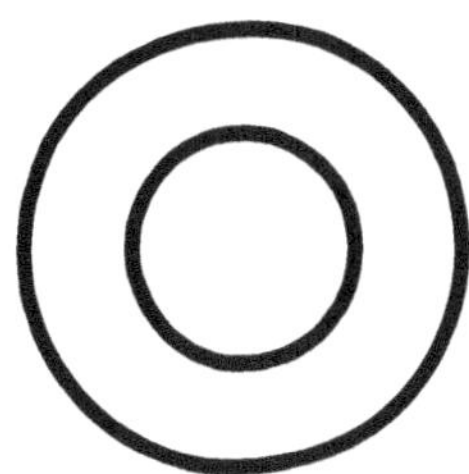

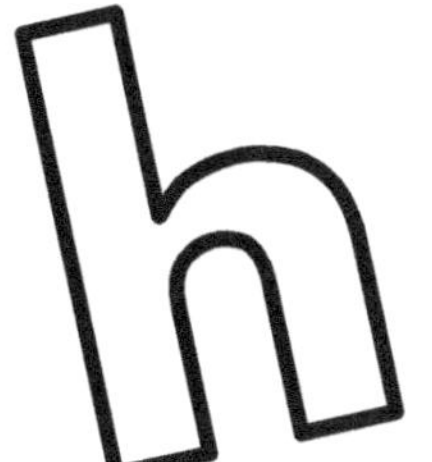 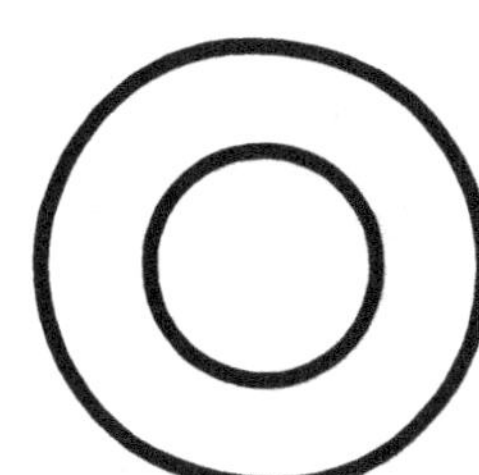 

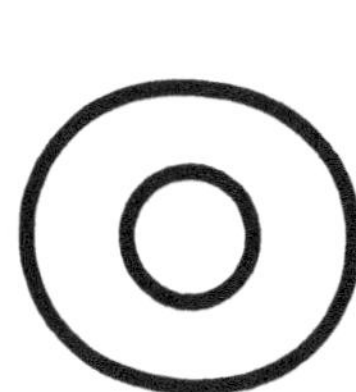 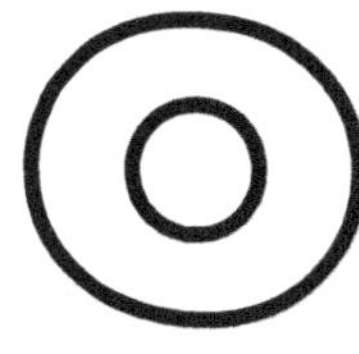 

I found the letter  __________ times.

Name: _______________

Oo

Word Search

orange
wopeno
looval

owl   oval

orange   open

Draw a line to help letter O get to letter P.

P p

P P P P P P P P P P P

p p p p p p p p p p p p

Name: ____________________

Words starting with **P p**

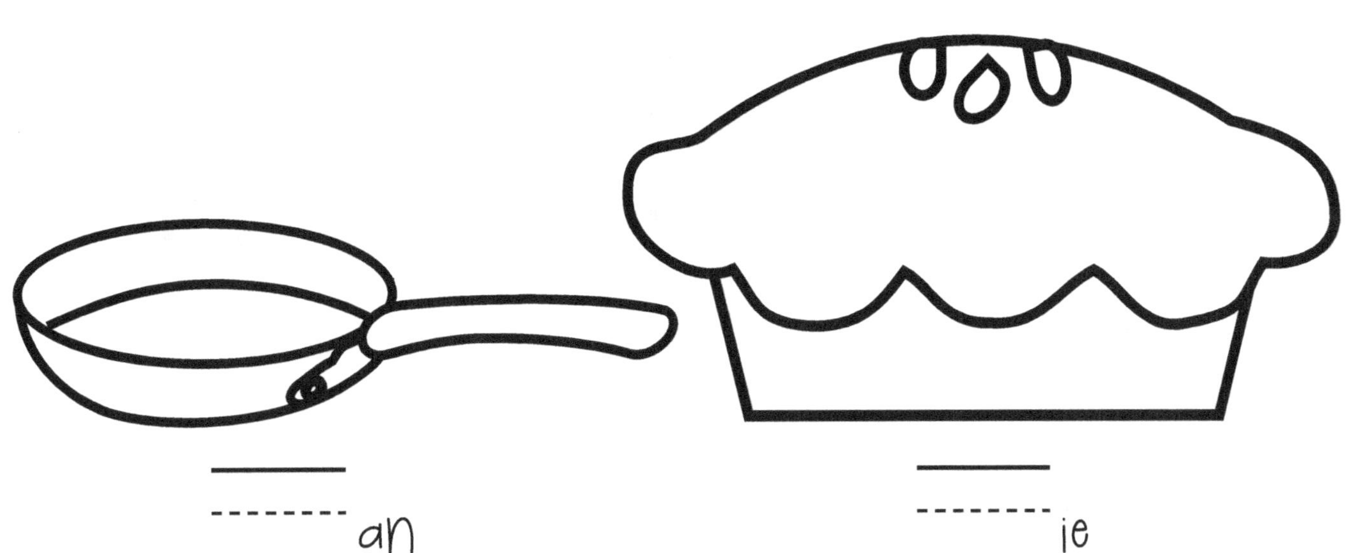

_____ izza

_____ encil

_____ an

_____ ie

Name: _______________________________

Color the letter 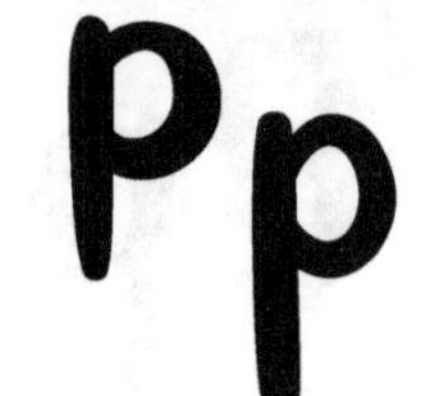

k N d

m  O 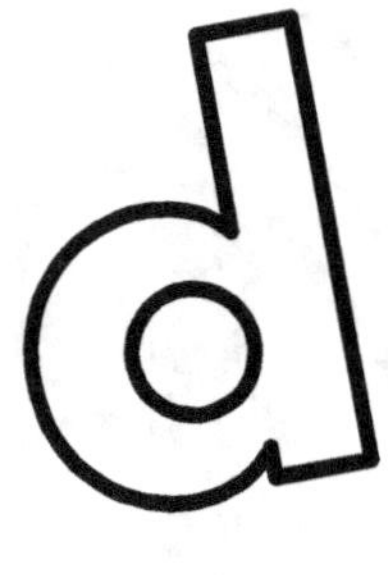 n

P M P

I found the letter  _______ times.

80

DressedInSheets

Name: _______________________

Pp

Word Search

p e n c i l
a p i z z a
n o p i e l

pizza   pencil

pan   pie

Draw a line to help letter P get to letter Q.

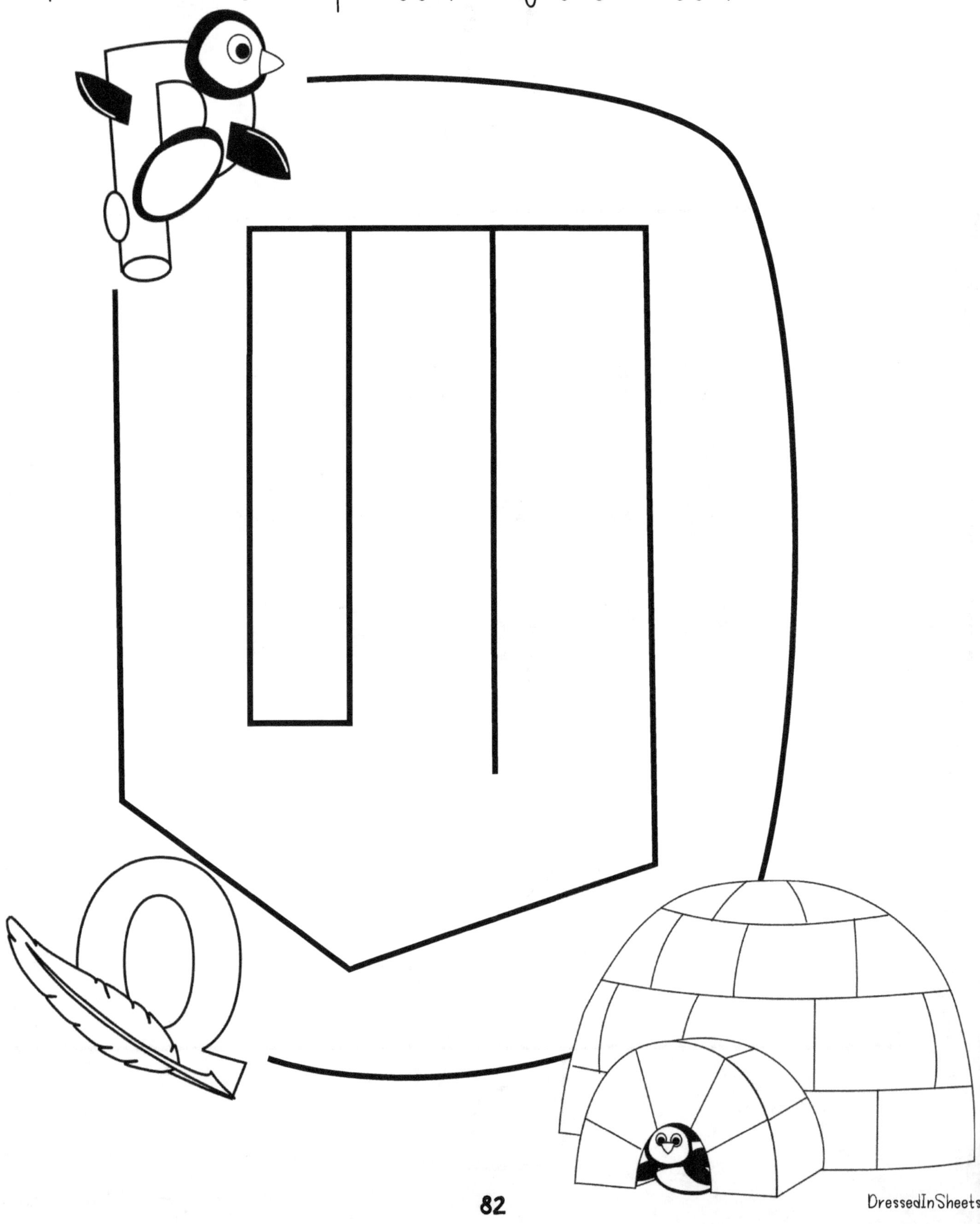

Name:

Q q

Words starting with **Qq**

Name: ___________________________________

Color the letter 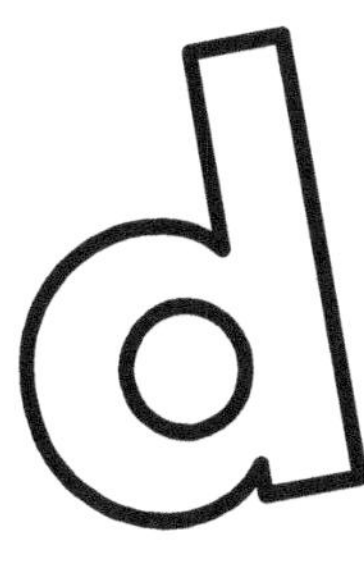

Q H d

m q Q

n q p

I found the letter  _________ times.

Qq

Word Search

q u e e n l a
q u i l l a s
q u a r t e r
a a q u i l t

queen   quilt

quill   quarter

Name: ___________________________

Draw a line to help letter Q get to letter R.

Name:

Rr

Words starting with **Rr**

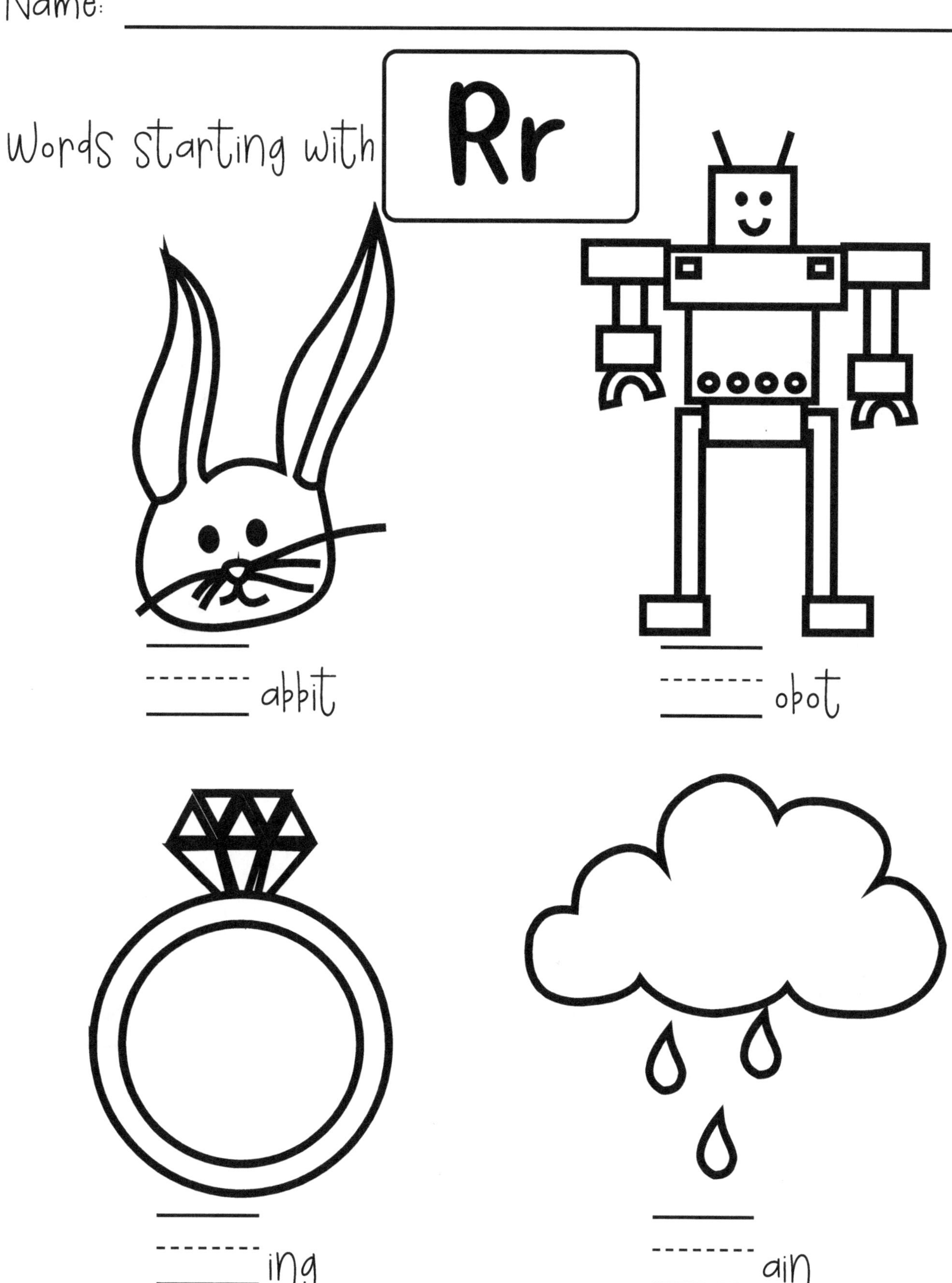

Name: ____

Color the letter **Rr**

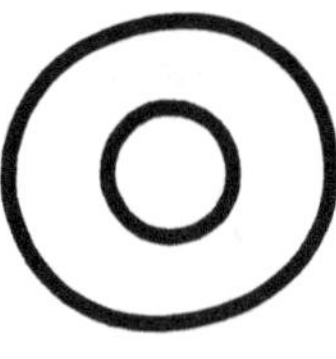

I found the letter **Rr** ___________ times.

Rr

Word Search

rabbit   rain

robot   ring

Name:

Draw a line to help letter R get to letter S.

Name: _______________________________

Ss

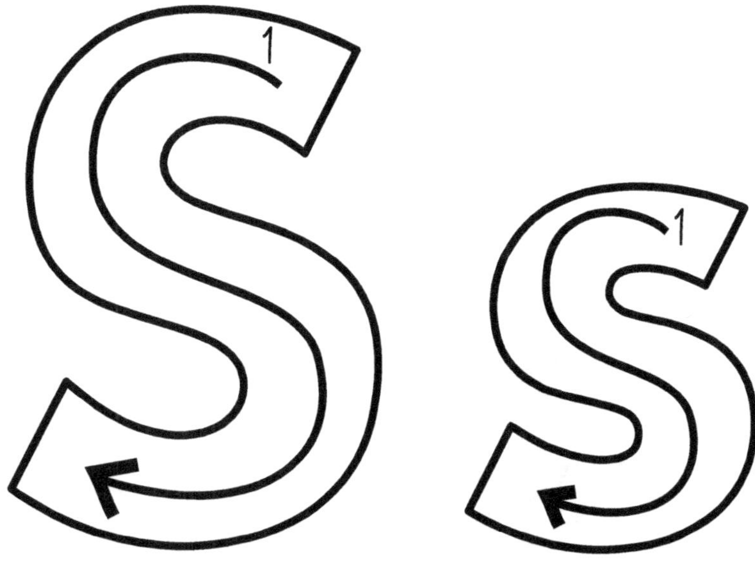

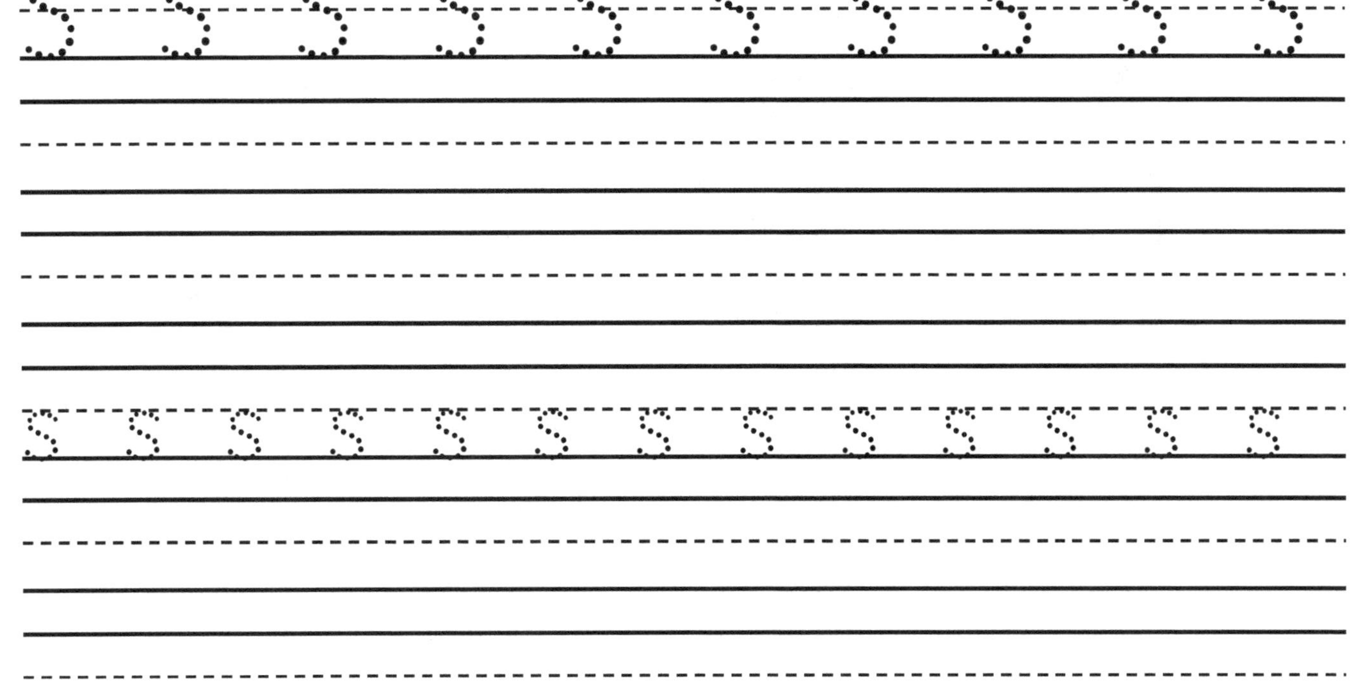

Name: ____

Words starting with **Ss**

_____ poon

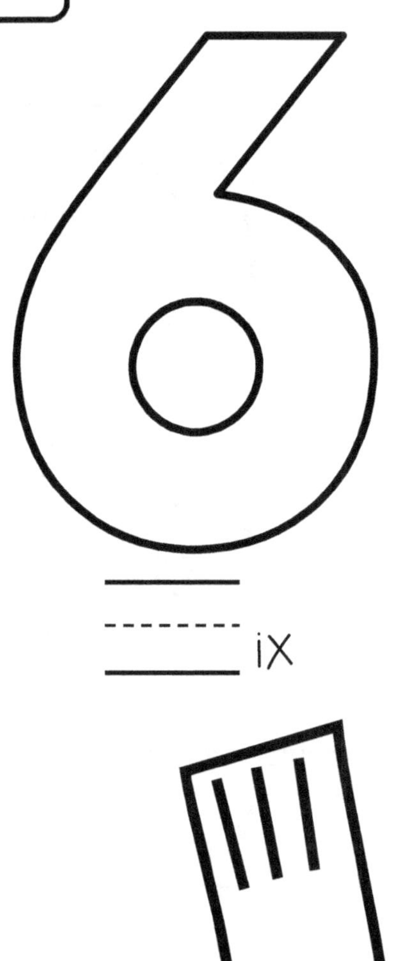

_____ ix

_____ un

_____ ock

Color the letter **Ss**

P r S

q e r

S  S

I found the letter **Ss**  times.

Ss

Word Search

s p o o n
a s i x s
i a r t u
s o c k n

spoon   six

sun   sock

Name: _______________________

Draw a line to help letter S get to letter T.

Name:

Tt

Words starting with **Tt**

___ able

___ wo

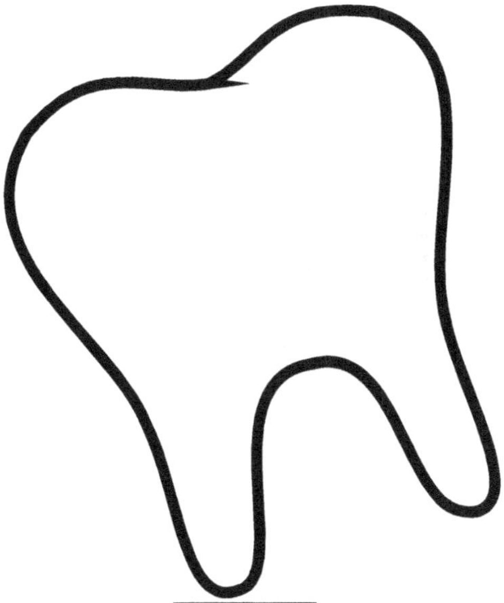

___ ooth

___ rain

Color the letter 

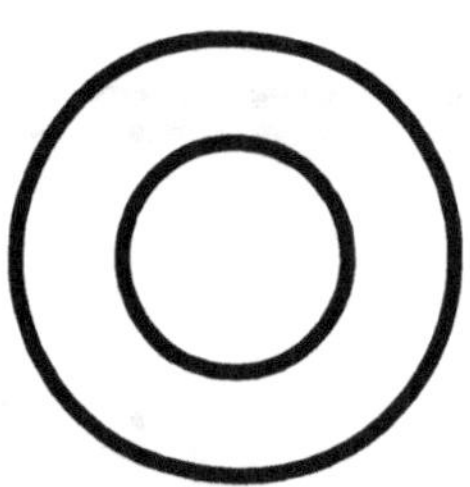

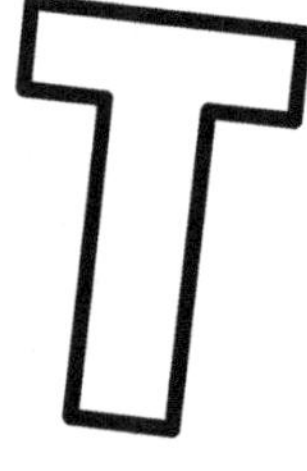

I found the letter 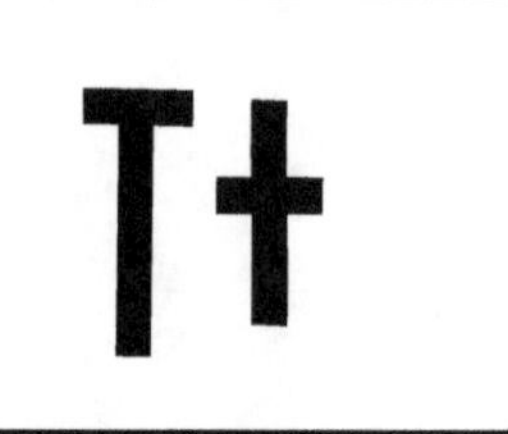 _______ times.

Tt

Word Search

t p t w o
t a b l e
t r a i n
t o o t h

table   two

tooth   train

Draw a line to help letter T get to letter U.

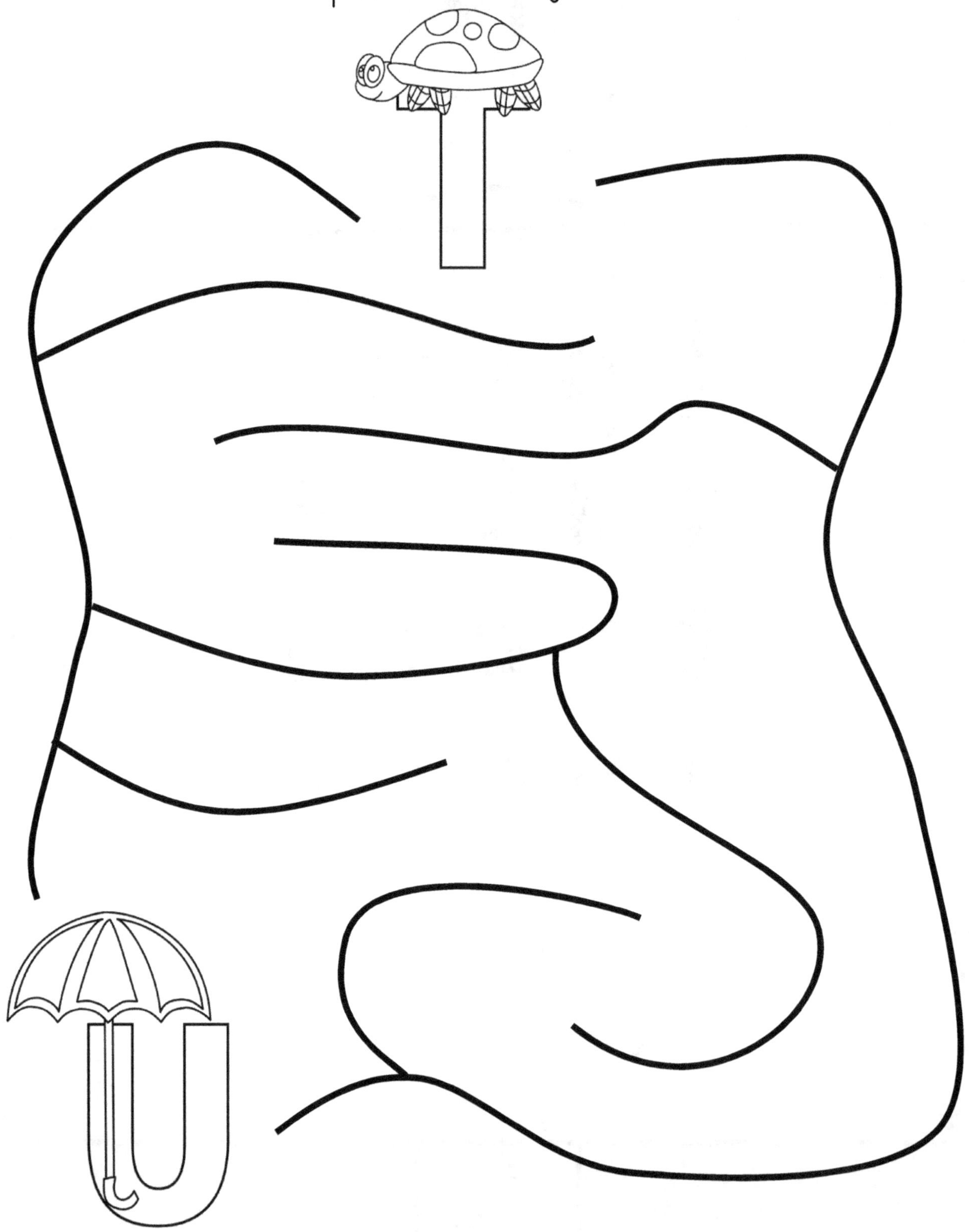

Uu

Words starting with 

_____ mbrella

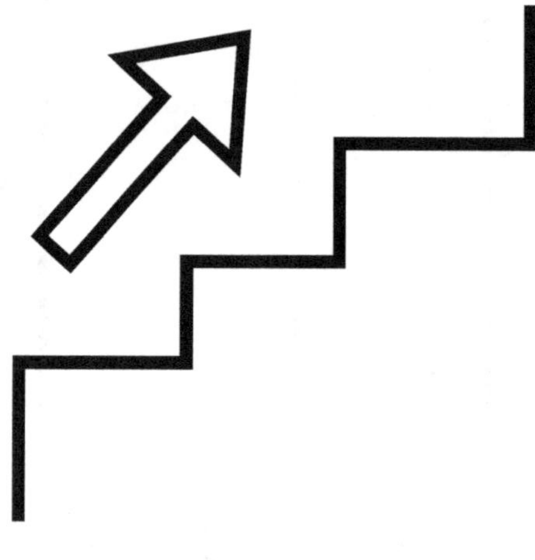

_____ p

_____ niform

_____ nhappy

Color the letter 

I found the letter  _______ times.

Uu

Word Search

u n h a p p y u
u n i f o r m p
u m b r e l l a

umbrella   up

uniform   unhappy

Name: ______________________________

Draw a line to help letter U get to letter V.

Name: _______________________

Vv

Name:
Words starting with   Vv 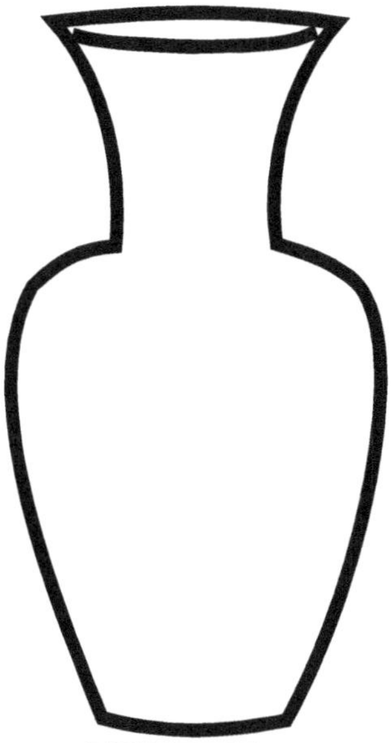
____ase 
____est 
____an 
____olcano

Name: ___________________________

Color the letter 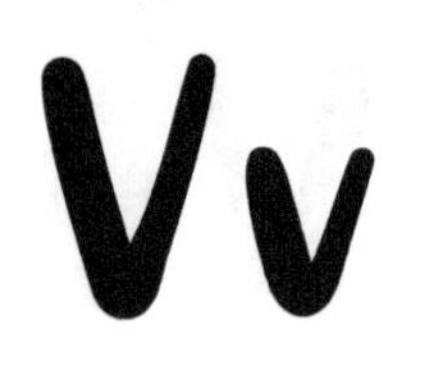

I found the letter 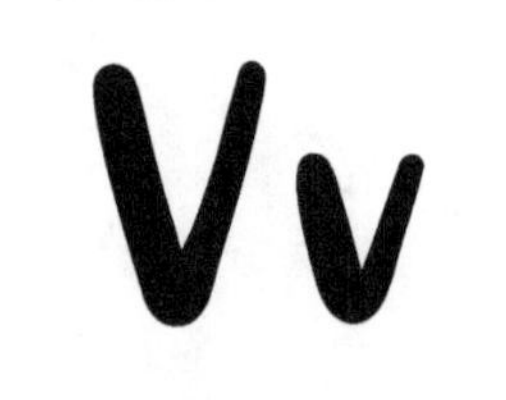 ___________ times.

Name: ____________________

Vv

Word Search

n h a v a s e
v o l c a n o
v e s t v a n

vase   van

vest   volcano

Draw a line to help letter V get to letter W.

Name: _______________________

Ww

Name: ____________________________

Words starting with W w

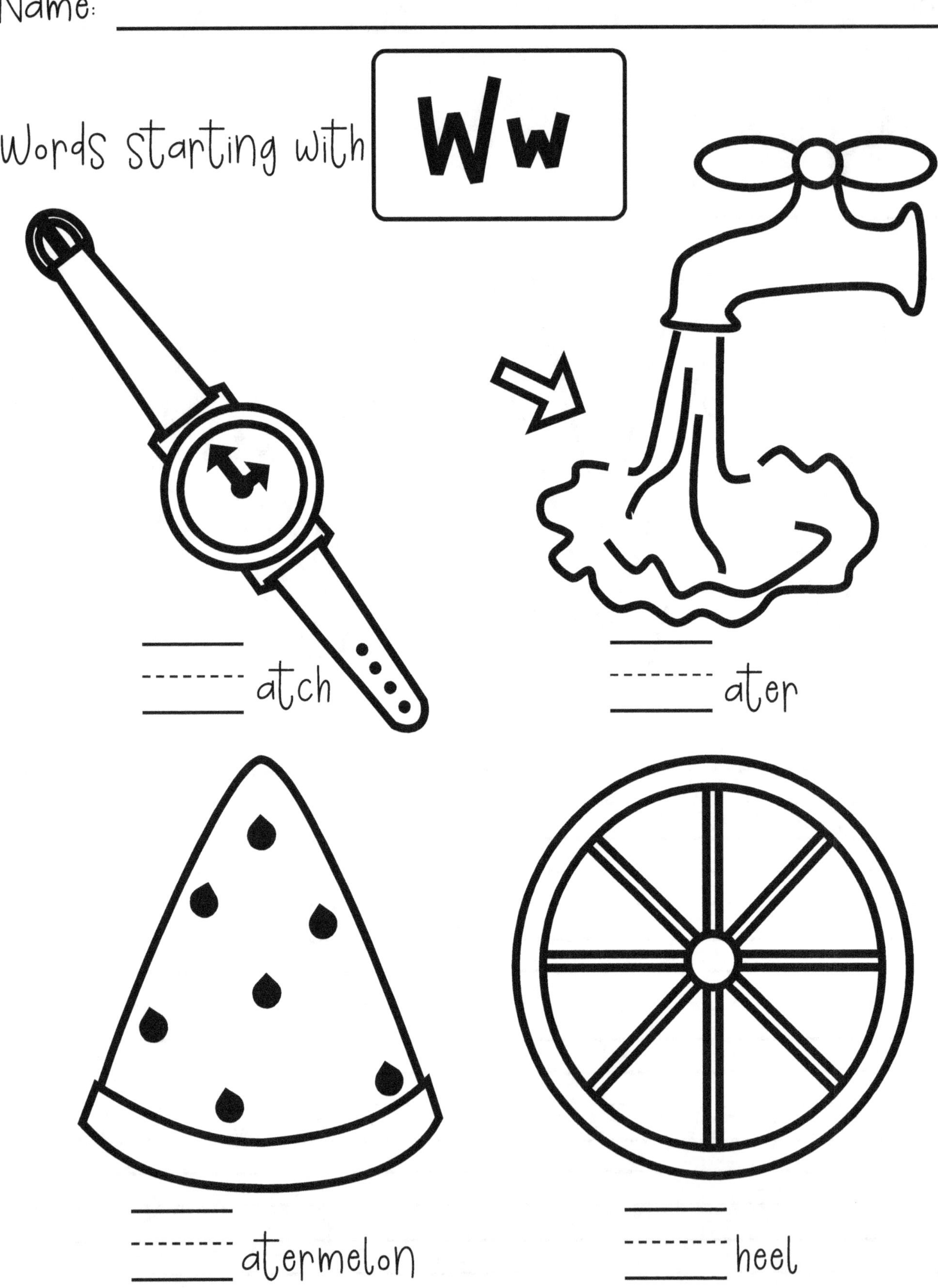

Name: ____

Color the letter 

I found the letter  _____________ times.

Name:

Ww

Word Search

watermelon
watchwheel
cbwaternzi

watch   water

watermelon   wheel

Draw a line to help letter W get to letter X.

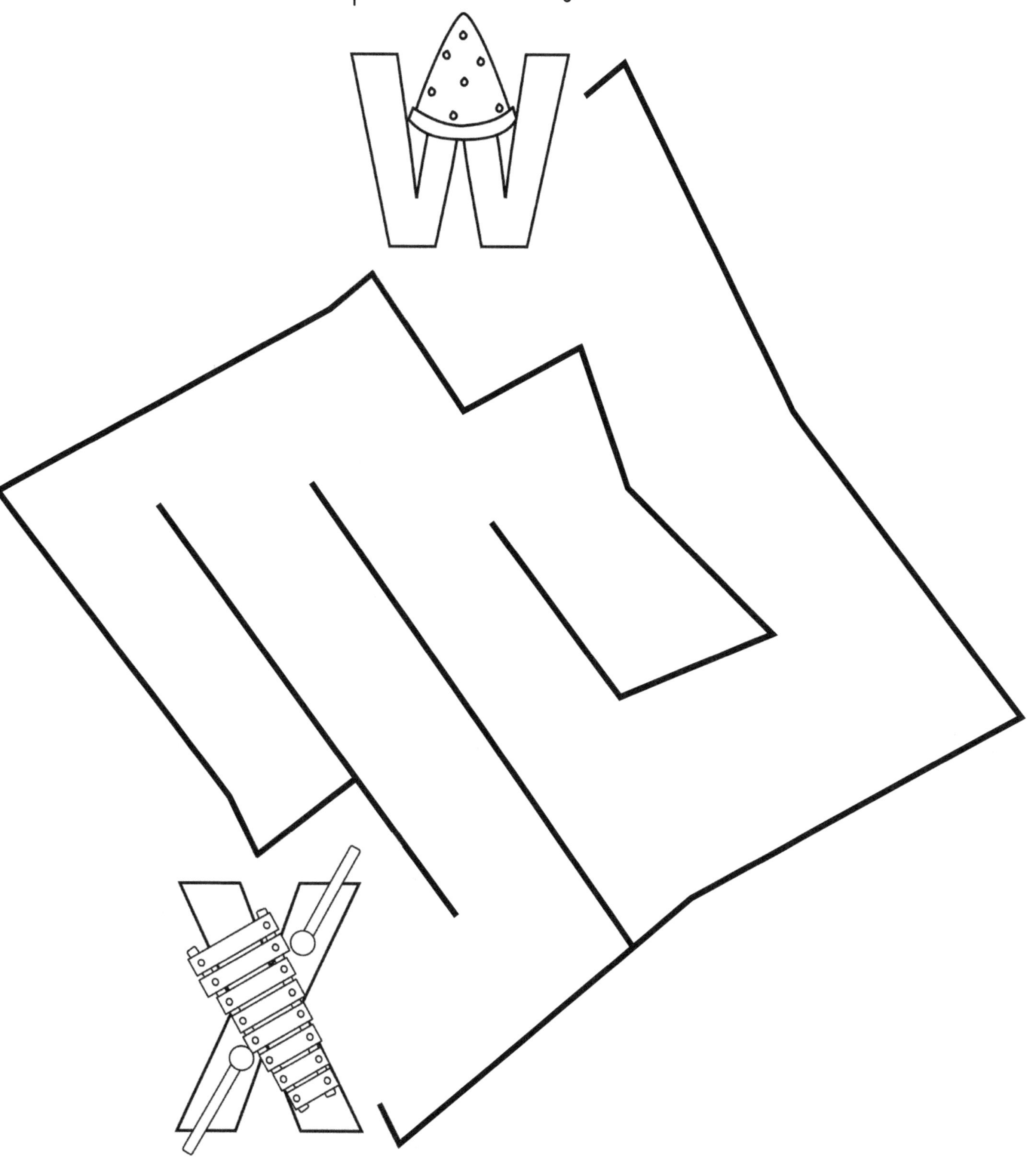

Name:

Xx

Name: _______________________

Words starting with **Xx**

_____-ray

_____ylophone

Write the words below.

xylophone _______________________

x-ray _______________________

Name: ___________________________________

Color the letter 

x   S   X

c   T   s

b   a   X

I found the letter  _________ times.

120

DressedInSheets

Draw a line to help letter X get to letter Y.

Yy

Name: _______________________

Words starting with **Yy**

_______olk

_______o-yo

Write the words below.

yo-yo _______________________

yolk _______________________

Color the letter 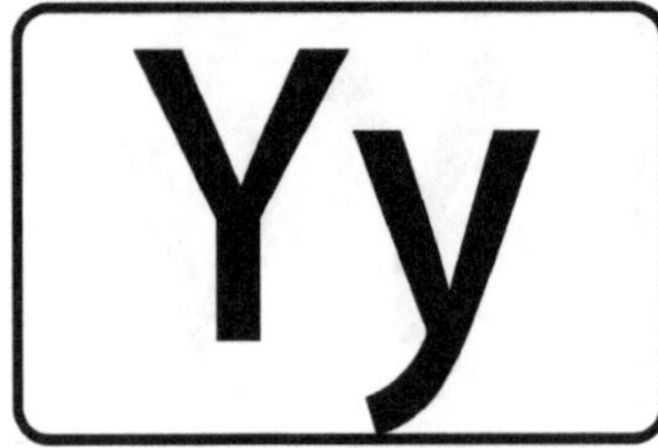

  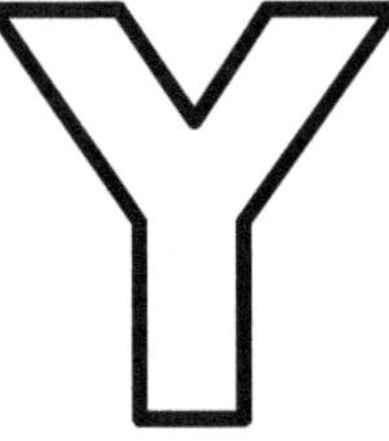

I found the letter 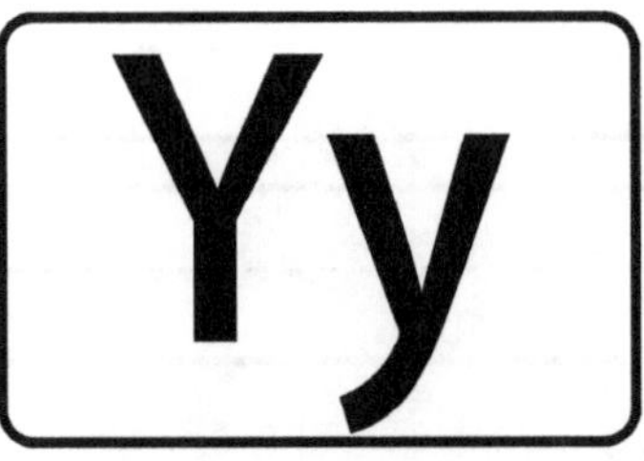 __________ times.

DressedInSheets

Draw a line to help letter Y get to letter Z.

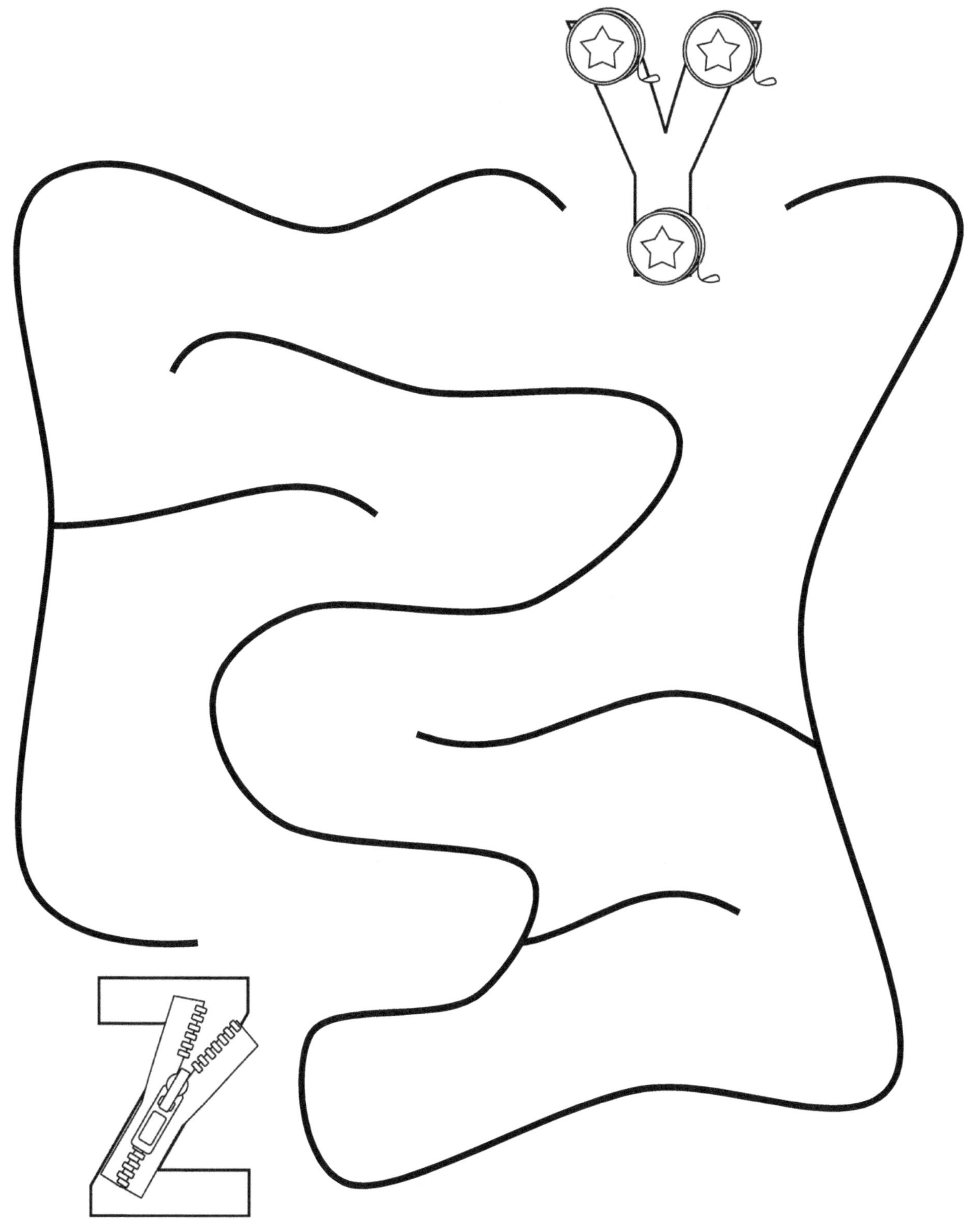

Name:
Zz

Words starting with **Zz**

______ero

______ipper

Write the words below.

zipper

zero

Color the letter **Zz**

I found the letter **Zz** __________ times.

Name: _______________________________   Date: _______________________

Practicing my writing

Name:_______________________   Date:_______________________

Practicing my writing